CONTENTS

Beautiful city of Edinburgh!
Where the tourist can drown his sorrow
By viewing your monuments and statues fine
During the lovely summer-time.

Beautiful city of Edinburgh! The truth to express,
Your beauties are matchless I must confess
And which no-one dare gainsay,
But that you are the grandest city in Scotland at the present day.

William McGonagall, **Poetic Gems**

VICTORIAN EDINBURGH: INTRODUCTION

Robert Louis Stevenson's Edinburgh was as two faced as Dr Jekyll and Mr Hyde. In the new town it had some of the most gracious architecture in Europe. But it also had in the Old Town and Calton some of the worst slums. Middle-class private housing was being built at a remarkable rate in Grange, Merchiston and other suburbs, but more than half of the city's families lived in one or two-room tenement flats, most without even basic amenities. There were churches and famous preachers everywhere; Alexander Whyte and Horatius Bonar, with new buildings in plenty, but as well as piety, Edinburgh had more than its fair share of prostitution. When illegitimacy statistics first became available in the late 1850's, they showed that Edinburgh's situation at 10% of all live births was worse than Glasgow's, even if not in the same league as Aberdeen. The city had many of the most able medical men in the country, such as Dr Littlejohn, the first Medical Officer of Health, but there was still large-scale infant mortality and despite some improvement, one in three deaths in the early 1890's was of a child under five. Schedule D income tax returns for 1880 showed Edinburgh to have more high earning individuals than anywhere in the United Kingdom save London and Manchester, thanks to its successful professions and businesses. But there were also many tens of thousands of poorly paid domestic servants, washerwomen, and seamstresses, street cleaners and flower sellers, plus an unknown number of casual workers; house painters, labourers and porters, who all too often had time on their hands to watch the prosperous go by. And there were the poor, who eked out an existence somehow, assisted to some extent by the many private charities of which the City boasted — or in extremis — by parochial relief. All British cities shared these problems, but in Victorian Edinburgh the contrast seems to have been more blatant than in most.

But whatever the realities of life for the residents, visitors found Edinburgh a fascinating place. Ever since the railways had opened up large scale tourism in Britain, Edinburgh had exercised a disproportionate appeal. Certainly none of the many Victorian guidebooks would have had it any other way, given its many attractions. A. & C. Black were an Edinburgh firm and therefore not entirely unbiased, but their **Picturesque Tourist of Scotland** (1866 edition) was not treading on controversial ground with the assertion that the great majority of tourists visiting Scotland came to Edinburgh first; **"its site is generally admitted to be unequalled in panoramic splendour by any capital in Europe"**. Though some might urge the claims of Athens or Constantinople, most British guides were of the same mind as Baddeley of the famed **Through Guides**; "Edinburgh is without doubt the finest city in the Kingdom" (**Scotland, Part I, 1903 edition**). As an Englishman writing for a London publisher, his assessment may be taken as reasonably impartial.

What visitors loved was the combination of history, architecture and views. The Castle and the Royal Mile were then, as now, great attractions. And there were the Galleries, Museums and Gardens, Churches, Monuments and Statues. Even the graveyards had their appeal to the Victorians. The Border Abbeys were within striking range, as were castles like Roslin, and Craigmillar, houses such as Hawthornden and Abbotsford. You could cycle, or take a carriage round the Queen's Drive to Dunsappie and St Margaret's Loch. The Forth Bridge, that marvel of Victorian engineering, was much inspected during construction by curious parties from Edinburgh. In short, the City catered for every taste; historical, literary or geological, excursionist, sporting enthusiast or simple tourist. And to accommodate visitors, old hotels were renovated and new hotels built, some forty odd between 1860 and 1910, the most famous of which were (and are) the Railway Companies' flagship symbols; the North British completed in 1902, and the rival Caledonian finished the following year. Most of the new hotels were, as ever, in and around Princes Street, but a few were further out such as the Braid Hills Hotel (1886) which claimed in its advertising that there were "Seventeen golf courses within a radius of fourteen miles" (**Caledonian Railway Summer Tours in Scotland, 1900**). The tourist was offered in Edinburgh every type of accommodation; there were the first-class hotels, Family and Tourist, Commercial and Temperence, with charges ranging from 5/- a night in the best establishments to much lower in the lesser. For the health conscious there was the hydropathic, the Craiglockhart (1886) complete with baths and resident physician.

The tourist trade benefited a wide range of Edinburgh people, even though the season was relatively short. Restauranteurs, shopkeepers — particularly those offering Scottish goods — lemonade salesmen, cabmen and hotel staff all looked to the summer visitor, and no group was more interested than the photographic fraternity who prepared postcards, views and albums for their clientele amongst the tourists. Edinburgh had been a centre of early experimentation with photography, and in the 1840's David Octavius Hill and Robert Adamson had been in the van of the new art.

By mid century, photography had begun to move out of doors, and to focus on scenes and views as well as portraits and cartes-de visite. By 1867 there were some 46 photographic artists at work in Edinburgh, including such well-known enterprises as James Howie's business at 60 Princes Street and the Rock Studios of Alexander Burns, later Alexander Inglis. Edinburgh photographers did not, however, have a monopoly of their home market in the provision of views. Valentine's of Dundee offered fierce competition, as did the firm whose photographs we are using in this book, G. W. Wilson & Co. of Aberdeen.

It is perhaps worth taking some time to sketch in the biography of George Washington Wilson (1823-1893), one of the greatest Victorian photographers, whose reputation has been in eclipse for many years but is of late enjoying a deserved revival. George Washington Wilson came of poor crofting stock in Banffshire, and by the time he was twenty-one had fathered two illegitimate children; Alexander Johnstone who became a successful journalist, and Robert who emigrated to New Zealand. George Washington Wilson had considerable artistic skills, and was sent to Edinburgh in the mid 1840's to further his ability as a portrait painter. But there he came into contact with photography, then being introduced as an adjunct to portraiture, and when he set up in

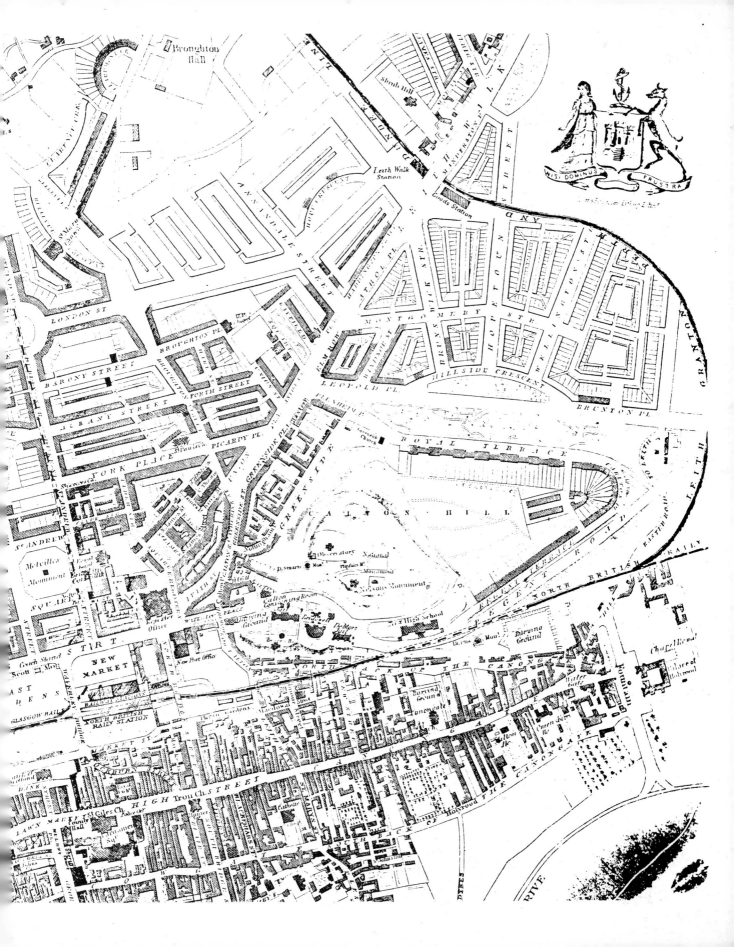

ALASTAIR DURIE

BRIAN KILOH

ALASTAIR DURIE was born, bred and educated in Edinburgh. After eighteen years at the University of Aberdeen, latterly as Senior Lecturer in Economic History and Director of the Overseas Office, he has just (1989) moved to the University of Glasgow preferring, however, to settle in Stirling from which he commutes. He has written extensively on Victorian photography and George Washington Wilson and numbers amongst his interests church, squash, and shooting, almost anything rather than work.

BRIAN KILOH is an Aberdonian who studied photography at Napier College in Edinburgh and has since been working as a professional photographer. Involved previously in a companion volume **Vanishing Aberdeen**, he enjoys sport and is that rare person who can.list amongst his hobbies the thing that he makes his living at — namely photography.

VANISHING EDINBURGH

in the steps of
George Washington Wilson

ALASTAIR J. DURIE

Modern Photography
by
Brian Kiloh

Keith Murray Publications

Aberdeen University Library

Published by Keith Murray Publications,
46 Portal Crescent, Tillydrone, Aberdeen, Scotland. AB2 2SP
in association with
Aberdeen University Library, Queen Mother Library, Meston Walk, Aberdeen AB9 2UE

First published 1989

Printed by The Acorn Press, Carnoustie, Scotland

ISBN 1 870978 12 9

Cover Designed by Innes Taylor, 1989

Aberdeen in the 1850's it was as an artist and photographer. His career received considerable assistance from royal patronage, initially in the form of a commission to photograph the rebuilding of Balmoral castle in 1853-4. This was to lead to a long association with Queen Victoria, underlined in his advertisement of himself as "Photographer to the Queen", a claim regularized by royal warrant in 1873, and by the granting of a cottage on Balmoral Estate for his holiday use. Royal patronage was important to Wilson's success, but so also was his technical skill. George Washington Wilson was one of the pioneers of "instantaneous photography", and some of his more significant early work was done in Princes Street. Showing as they did people and traffic in motion, these studies excited international comment, and not surprisingly Wilson was the only Scottish photographer to be awarded a medal in the London International Exhibition of 1862, puting several Edinburgh competitors into the shade.

Important though Royal patronage and technical skills were, at the centre of George Washington Wilson's success was his commercial acumen. Wilson's firm undertook portrait work in Aberdeen, from family groups to dead infants, but the largest and most profitable side of his business was the production of scenes and views, some individual, others bound in books. His market was the sightseer, and while he covered every part of Scotland which was on the tourist track, Edinburgh received a special attention. A volume entitled **Views of Edinburgh** which significantly sold at railway bookstalls and bookshops, was issued in 1865, and other editions appeared over the next decades. Even after Wilson retired from business in the late 1880's the firm continued to pay special attention to the city. Louis Wilson, George Washington Wilson's fourth son, who later worked as a photographer in Hawaii, took some 30 views of Edinburgh in the late 1890's and the firm bought in for lantern slide purposes views from Alexander Inglis in 1905. The George Washington Wilson catalogues, therefore, always held a full portfolio of Edinburgh views, reflecting both George Washington Wilson's personal knowledge of the city he had lived in for two years and revisited frequently, and the continuing demand from the market for Edinburgh material.

What we have in the George Washington Wilson archive held by Aberdeen University is a record of Edinburgh built up over forty years, from the late 1850's to just after the turn of the century. Many of the firm's plates and slides were lost when it slid into bankruptcy in 1907, and of the thousand or so views of Edinburgh we have less than half. But the surviving material is more than adequate in quality. Clearly given Wilson's commercial objective, the coverage is of the traditional tourist vistas, taken from such well-loved vantage points as the Calton Hill, the Scott Monument, the Castle and Arthur's Seat. No studies survive, alas, from the Pentlands, nor any from Corstorphine Hill. But there is ample evidence to vindicate George Washington Wilson's love of Edinburgh as a photographer: he wrote in his commentary on the first edition of **Edinburgh Views** that he found the "prospects from the elevated points of the city and neighbourhood one of singular beauty". And some of the photographs he took stand comparison with the best modern work, even if he had the time to make sure that the weather and light were always in his favour.

What can we learn from these Victorian views, and their present day counterparts? The Edinburgh that George Washington Wilson knew was itself changing rapidly, expanding to the North, South, East and West. True, even in 1900, it was far more compact than present-day Edinburgh, and far better served by public and private transport. There were tramways and cable cars, now gone completely; the horse cabs and carts; almost disappeared save for an occasional brewer's dray cart. The once-extensive network of suburban railways has shrivelled almost to nothing. Currie and Colinton, Barnton and Davidson's Mains, Trinity and Dalkeith, have alike lost their lines, and only freight moves through Morningside or to Leith, more's the pity. Horse transport had its drawbacks in terms of speed and smell but the current situation, as the photographs make clear, is one of over-congestion of the city by the motor-car.

It is interesting to speculate, were Wilson himself to return what would he find most different about the city. Mere change would not surprise him, I think. In his day there were losses through demolition or fires, such as the gutting of a tenement in North Bank Street in August 1857. There were the city improvement schemes which swept away old wynds in favour of new streets such as Chambers Street. There were the series of enlargements to Waverley Station. And, of course, there were the new churches, St Mary's Cathedral, for instance, which so dominated the West Central Area. He would notice today the abandonment of church buildings, the absence of any new statues, the alteration of shop fronts, the intrusion of the St James' Centre, the disappearance of most factory chimneys, the absence of smoke and smog. Yet a surprising number of retailer's names would be familiar to him.

And many of the salient features of the Victorian skyline are still present, and prominent, though some — like the Scott monument — are in need of a good clean. A problem for the modern-day photographer, as Brian Kiloh has found, is the tree line which in some places obscures the classical views. Edinburgh is still one of the most striking cities in the world, but we cannot merely take this for granted. Perhaps this book will help to point up what is distinctive and worthy of preservation. We need to know where we have been, and where we now are, to have some sense of where we should be.

Alastair Durie, September 1989

SELECT BIBLIOGRAPHY

Any of the many Victorian guidebooks Murray's **Handbook for Scotland**, Baddeley's **Through Guide**, Black's **Guide to Scotland**, or Patterson's **The Tourist Guide to Scotland** makes a delightful introduction to Victorian Edinburgh. Essential, however, is Gifford, McWilliam and Walker, **The Buildings of Scotland: Edinburgh** or Charles McKean; **Edinburgh, An Illustrated Architectural Guide**. Roger Taylor's **George Washington Wilson, Artist and Photographer** remains the standard work on George Washington Wilson.

ACKNOWLEDGEMENTS

This book owes much to the enthusiasm and skill of Aberdeen University Library's photographic unit, Mike Craig and Caroline Gilbert who did so much to bring the George Washington Wilson photographs up to their best. Mary Murray, as the person in charge of the George Washington Wilson archive, was as ever helpful far beyond the call of duty. Linda Logan found time amidst all her commitments to translate into typescript a hand that would have shamed any Victorian schoolchild, and my wife, Kate, commented and corrected with gusto!

All the GWW views are drawn from the Wilson Collection in Aberdeen University Library, and prints can be purchased of any of the photographs in this book by applying to the Queen Mother Library, Meston Walk, Aberdeen AB9 2UE citing the photographic reference.

NATIONAL GALLERY FROM THE MOUND c1860

It is perhaps difficult for us to appreciate how hostile many contemporaries were to the Mound. Sir Walter Scott described it as "the most helpless and irremediable error which has been committed in the course of the improvements of Edinburgh". He and others wanted a bridge. Thirty years after its completion in 1830 when two million cart loads of soil and rubbish had been dumped, the scene looks much better than the lumpish accumulation to which he objected. The newly built National Gallery gracefully complements the Royal Institution, and at least its grass is beginning to grow on the garden side of the Mound railings. An elderly woman pauses on her way up to the Old Town, and a child plays at the kerbside near the foot of the decline, something no-one would risk today, given the traffic. The skyline is not much changed but the flags of the Victorian Royal Hotel comfortably dwarf what is presently on offer. Notice the steps leading down into West Princes Street Gardens, one of the many walks laid out in the 1870's. To the relief of the drivers, the granite setts have gone.

EDINBURGH. FROM THE CASTLE. 151. G.W.W.

CASTLE TO CALTON HILL

Much is common to these two photographs, such as the Station, the Scott Monument and the Calton Hill, but closer examination throws up some interesting differences apart, of course, from the North British Hotel, so dominant on the site once occupied by Victorian shops such as Cránston & Elliot's Drapery. Princes Street Gardens no longer has sheep on it as it did in the 1860's. The trees everywhere have matured to mask the paths and base of the Scott Monument alike. Waverley Station was under evergrowing pressure in the later nineteenth century, particularly after the opening of the Forth Bridge, and it was remodeled in the 1890's to the station we see today. The Mound tunnel acquired an additional bore, as can be seen. To the right, Ramsay Gardens conceals the front of New College and the Bank of Scotland.

The gardens have a number of families sitting out or walking around, and to the left of the elegant Victorian greenhouses a group are waiting on the footbridge for the next train. The signals are all at halt, but it would not be long before a train passed. The engine's smoke and sparks might not have best suited the the children's clean clothes!

CASTLE TO THE NORTH

Dominating the view to the North is Fettes College, completed in 1870, and its boarding houses set amongst the largely green fields of Inverleith and Drylaw. To the left is the Combination Poorhouse of St Cuthbert's and Canongate, removed to this new site in 1866 after the previous property had been bought by the Caledonian Railway Company for its Lothian Road station. The New Town stands out very clearly, especially the elegant Royal Circus, Charlotte Square and behind the dome of St George's, Belgrave Terrace. Princes Street is still a mixture of private houses, clubs and some shops. Some soldiers lounge against the parapet of the battery which became the home of the one-o-clock gun, first fired from the Castle on the 26th of January 1861. The modern visitors find a clock mounted in the small turret, or would do if they were allowed into that area. Princes Street is all shops and stores with, one is glad to see, one awning at least. To the north, Fettes is in need of a complete clean amidst the trees, and the gasometers at Granton and the high rise flats of Pilton and elsewhere mark the northern limits of the city. Just visible is the Forth Rail Bridge over the dome of St George's.

MONS MEG

This famous late 15th century cannon was taken to the Tower of London in 1754 and only brought back in 1829 at the instigation of Sir Walter Scott, in conjunction with the visit to Edinburgh of George IVth. The gun carriage with its inscriptions was later replaced by something more appropriate to its age, although it has to be said that the Georgian carriage is very fine, as was the location beside St Margaret's Chapel at the Bomb Battery of the King's Bastion. The iron cannonball appears to have gone missing in the recent move to the vault where Meg is now protected from the weather. Mons Meg was one of the key attractions for the Victorians, along with the Regalia, and no fee was charged for admission to the Castle. A Military Band played every Sunday afternoon during the summer, a nice notion that could be revived.

CASTLE ESPLANADE

In what appears to be a full parade of the 2nd battalion of the Gordon Highlanders c1890, the officers and NCOs are fully occupied, apart from the platoon nearest the camera whose participation in the proceedings appears to have been suspended. The newly completed drawbridge and gate-house which look so authentic, were the gift of the publisher William Nelson in 1887. Sir Douglas Haig's statue (1923) the last to be erected anywhere in Edinburgh, looks out now over the Esplanade. Keen and brave cavalryman as he was, his thinking and tactics were more appropriate to Victorian warfare than that of World War One. But one wonders how many of the passers by make any connection between him and the registers of the dead in the Castle's Hall of Honour?

OUTWORK AND SENTRY

The piles of timber to the right and Cameron & Co's winch suggest a date of 1886 or 1887 when the Castle Entrance was reconstructed, replacing a much less impressive outwork.

ESPLANADE

The Esplanade was a favourite place for the citizens of Victorian Edinburgh. Here a group have gathered to watch the troops at drill, while a cart waits for admission to the castle. The gentleman nearest the camera has on a smart pair of check trousers and his magnificent black hound seems quite content to wait in the afternoon sun. Nowadays, visitors to the Esplanade are more likely to be from overseas, and armed with their own cameras. Any troops wishing to drill would have little room for manoeuvre with all the cars and buses. The Army presence is marked still by a Scots Guards' Landrover in front of the Ticket Office for the Tattoo. But how many locals ever find their way to the Esplanade?

ESPLANADE TO THE SOUTH-EAST

Some of the worst housing in Victorian Edinburgh lay in and around the Grassmarket. Greyfriars Church stands out clearly, as do many of the tombstones so beloved by Victorian photographers and to the left is the roof of the Chambers Street Museum of Science and Art opened in 1866, to which admission was free (by some curious logic) on Wednesdays and weekends. At other times it cost 6d to get in to see the fossils and other exhibits. To the left is the Edinburgh Normal School, which trained female teachers; in the intervening years, close study reveals the building to have acquired an additional line of windows on the west side! The greatest contrast is in the Grassmarket area where there is so much new or renovated housing. A few of the older properties remain and even the odd row of chimneys, but it is a greatly improved environment. Beyond Greyfriars can be seen the University of Edinburgh's Appleton and David Hume Towers.

ESPLANADE, LOOKING TOWARDS TOLBOOTH CHURCH

The esplanade is almost deserted, save for two or three elderly gentlemen enjoying the sun. Frederick, Duke of York's Statue is nearest the camera: then comes a cross commemorating officers and men of the 78th Highlanders killed during the Indian Mutiny, and finally a memorial to Colonel MacKenzie of the 92nd Highlanders. Other statues were to be added subsequently with Earl Haig's completing the line-up: all have their pedestals boxed up prior to the Tattoo stands being erected. Cannonball house is still here to the head of Castlehill, but the adjoining Military and Naval Institute has long since moved away. Short's Observatory where visitors went to view the town, not the skies, has become the Camera Obscura. The most striking difference is Ramsay Gardens designed by Professor Patrick Geddes in the 1890's and constructed in a fascinating mixture of styles. Some of us were allowed in our youth to watch the Tattoo from there for free. Mind you, the residents themselves would say they pay a high price for that privilege as the programme is repeated night after night.

AUL F848

OUTSIDE CANNONBALL HOUSE

Two loafers lean over a wall at the head of the steps while an elderly and well-laden man pauses to stare curiously towards George Washington Wilson and his camera. The only audience that the video camera-man outside the car park's ticket booth has is his son, although there are plenty of sightseers about.

THE WEST BOW

The woollen and rag store in the delapidated tenement on the corner of the West Bow was soon to be demolished and rebuilt. Its presence was another sign, if one were needed, of the poverty of this area which had long since been abandoned by the upper and middle classes. Next door is a second-hand furniture shop; across the road one of the many pawnshops. Yet the inhabitants had not lost heart entirely. There are flower boxes on the window ledges and cages with canaries to brighten up their rooms. At the right hand side is the Free Church's response to St John's, also completed in 1845. St Columba's was a church which offered services in Gaelic to cater for immigrant Highlanders, mostly girls working in Edinburgh as domestic servants. In 1891 as well as the 4715 people who spoke both Gaelic and English there were reportedly 15 who spoke only Gaelic. One wonders how they coped. The wayside pulpit is today in English. The tenements of the West Bow are undergoing renovation, a welcome alternative to the post war policy of demolition.

HIGHLAND ST JOHN'S CHURCH

The rivalry following the Disruption of 1843 produced a surge of church-building in mid-Victorian Scotland. Otherwise known as the Tolbooth Church, St John's foundation stone was laid by Queen Victoria herself and completed in 1844 to the design of Gillespie Graham and A. W. N. Pugin for a total cost of £16,000 which seems not unreasonable for a grand building with elegant interior, spire of 241 feet, and an Assembly Hall able to house the General Assembly of the Church of Scotland which moved there in preference to its previous cramped venue in St Giles Cathedral. But as with so many other inner-city churches, the congregation dwindled in the twentieth century, and when the Assembly moved elsewhere, the writing was on the wall. The end came in 198 since when the building has lain empty, although the open door and builders offices seem to suggest some activity. At least Edinburgh does not seem to have as yet experienced the kind of astonishing conversions that some redundant kirk buildings in Aberdeen for example have undergone to warehouses, pubs and restaurants, and private flats. The fault is really that of the Victorians who simply built too many churches.

CITY CHAMBERS AND MARKET CROSS

The old market cross, or mercat croce, has had a chequered existence since its first erection. Demolished in 1756 on the ground that it was a hazard to traffic, the shaft rested for nearly a century in the grounds of Drum House before being brought back to St Giles. W. E. Gladstone, then MP for Midlothian and Prime Minister, paid for its restoration in 1885 with a new base tower and unicorn on top of the shaft. Around the parapet are eight coats of arms including those of the City, Canongate and University, not that the children in front are the least interested. What is striking is how all the shops, to say nothing of the Royal Exchange Hotel have now disappeared. Gone is Peter Slavin the slater's premises, along with the lums on display above the doorway. Gone also is Hardie's hat store at 289, all to allow free access through the arches to the City Chambers. The gas lamps of Parliament Square have given way to 'No Waiting' signs and litter bins. Intriguingly, whereas most places have lost their railings, the tree at the corner of the square has cast-iron protection.

CASTLE FROM JOHNSTON TERRACE

A fine and familiar view this, which has changed remarkably little over the years. Our sympathy in the Victorian scene has to lie with the cart-horse toiling up the brae. It looks as the load is a piano, perhaps from Jupp's in Lothian Road. Spare a thought for the modern day father lifting a pram up the Castlehill steps.

ST GILES CATHEDRAL

We can guess that it was with pride and relief that the minister of St Giles waited at the door to welcome the Queen's Commissioner to the General Assembly. Tuesday 23rd May 1883 was set as the day for a service to mark the completion of the renovation of the interior of St Giles, and 3000 invited guests waited inside for the proceedings to begin. And what was even better for Dr Lees was that the works to the choir, nave and transept were all paid for by the Edinburgh publisher, Dr William Chambers, who had been distressed by the muddle of St Giles which in the mid-nineteenth century was shared by no less than three congregations; the High, Old and West. True, though there was a new West door, the statues of the monarchs and ministers which were intended to grace the surrounding niches had not yet been finished, but otherwise everything was in place, including an organ. It was a pity, however, that only a few days previously Dr Chambers had died at the ripe old age of 83. As the Earl of Aberdeen's carriage arrives watching are a good crowd, several coachmen and from the roof some of the workmen. St Giles' continues to be both an historic kirk and a place of worship, but the emptiness of County Square suggests that this is not a Sunday. It is a suggestive comment on how little some church practice has altered in a century that in 1883 the churchgoer could count on Services at 11.30 am and 6.30 pm. The West congregation, incidentally were given a new building on the other side of the Meadows.

GEORGE IV BRIDGE

Holy Corner Morningside is said to be the most densely churched part of Edinburgh but the east end of George IV Bridge must run it close with Augustine Bristo Congregational Church to the left, the North Free Church (later the Edinburgh University Chaplaincy) at the junction of Bristo Place and Forrest Road, the Evangelical Union church (later Elim Pentecostal) opposite, and Greyfriars just out of sight. The church buildings all still survive, although the Congregational Church pinnacles have lost some of their iron work. The biggest difference is the arrival of the National Library of Scotland, which took over fifteen years to complete thanks to the Second World War. It took the place of the orthodoxly elegant County Buildings and its railings. Across the road in c1870 some building work was in progress, to judge from the hoardings and cart.

EDINBURGH PUBLIC LIBRARY

Many, if not most, of Scotland's public libraries in the later nineteenth century were partially or wholly financed by Andrew Carnegie. He himself laid the foundation stone of Edinburgh's Public Library on the 9th July 1887, and the building duly opened three years later at a cost to Carnegie of £50,000 — with some 75,000 volumes. This, of course, was not the first library in Edinburgh as there were the law libraries, the private circulating libraries and the collections belonging to various working men's institutes, but the public library offered general access to all, a principle it has maintained over the years even though the nature of its book holdings must now be much more diversified than merely the improving and the instructive. Little has changed in the exterior and above the door of the adjoining building which was formerly the premises of the Highland and Agricultural Society is still the group depicting Caledonia and her children. Further north behind the scaffolding is Lothian Regional Council's 1968 building.

VICTORIA STREET

Itself a new street laid out in the late 1820's to link the Grassmarket with George IV Bridge, Victoria Street and the Terrace above possessed many charming features, not least the many small shops. According to the 1885 Postal Directory, there were tinsmiths, tea merchants, ironmongers and hatters, to say nothing of the Primitive Methodist Chapel (Ebenezer Chapel) and the Edinburgh Mechanics Subscription Library, which had some 600 members in 1880, paying 6/- a year for membership.

Across the road at No 1 Victoria Street, the India Buildings accommodated the North British Lactina Manufacturing Company, a dairying enterprise or so one assumes and a branch of the British Linen Bank. A hundred years later all the records of the 'BL' were gathered in the Bank of Scotland Library located there, the British Linen having been taken over in 1971. Otherwise little has changed, save the arrival of the Regional Building at the corner, and the substitution of tarmac for granite setts.

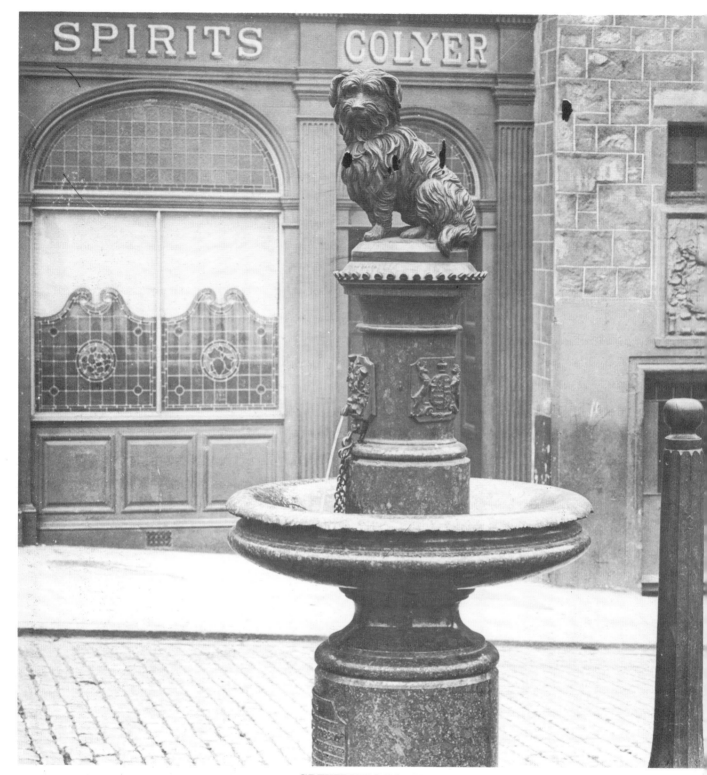

GREYFRIARS BOBBY

Few stories of animal faithfulness are better known than that of the Greyfriars Bobby, a Skye Terrier said to have died of grief on it
master's grave in the adjoining Greyfriars Churchyard, but who somehow took fourteen years about it! Baroness Bartlett Burdett
Coutts commisioned this statue in 1871, and received the freedom of the City for this and other good works in 1874. She seems to
have been a formidable lady, with taste for good causes at home and abroad, such as an Irish Fisheries Scheme to relieve
unemployment and a Turkish Compassionate Fund. The fountain no longer provides any water but for those of the Greyfriar
congregation smitten with a thirst after righteousness, a hostelry is available, and long has been, nearby in Candlemaker Row
Notice the coat of arms panel above the doorway of the Candlemakers' Hall, an early eighteenth century building.

GRASSMARKET c1865

That this was the carters' headquarters in the Old Town is underlined by the carts and horses, tackle and hay lining the kerb side.
From the Beehive (number 20) left weekly carts to Dalkeith, West Linton, Prestonkirk and other places, although an increasing
amount of the longer distance traffic was being taken over by the railways. At least the Beehive's roof was in better condition than
that of its near neighbour, the Black Bull. On the other side is one of the few snuff manufacturers left in the town; their numbers were
down to a mere half dozen or so by the 1860's. Above the Grassmarket looms the Castle, less changed save for the unlamented loss
of an externally mounted privy than any other aspect of this scene nowadays. The Beehive as remodeled in 1868 remains, as does
the Black Bull and the tenement, but number 22 (Williamson's Tobacco and Snuff Manufacturing) has been consolidated into the
Beehive, and the marvellous pipe-smoking figurehead lost. Partially concealed behind the trees to the left is Robertson Memorial
Church of 1884, a mission church which failed. Drink does better than religion in the Grassmarket.

THE VENNEL

Edinburgh has many such small steep streets called in this case the vennel from the old french root 'vennelle'. Not a particularly attractive alley, the vennel was home to the United Presbyterians' Portsburgh Church, long since disused, and a Ragged Feeding School known as New Greyfriars, one of a dozen or so institutions designed to feed, clothe and educate children from very poor homes. A group of children is to be seen at the Grassmarket entrance. A through road in the nineteenth century, it must have been little used by carters, and it has very sensibly now been pedestrianised. The trees to the left now obscure some of the potentially fine views of the Castle where the 1887 Gatehouse is clearly visible.

JOHN KNOX'S HOUSE

All the nineteenth century guidebooks steered visitors to this interesting sixteen century house without ever questioning the accepted wisdom that it had belonged to John Knox and that he had preached to crowds from the upper window. Modern historians are more sceptical. Nevertheless it still does a roaring trade. The frontages are painted up, as is the figure of John Knox in the act of preaching. The house in fact came close to demolition in 1849 when it was condemned by the Town Council as unsafe but its supposed connection saved it. Less has been done for the well which was once an important source of water for the inhabitants of the Royal Mile. You can see how in Wilson's photograph the steps are wet and worn, and while the children have caps or hats, they are without shoes.

AUL C3903x

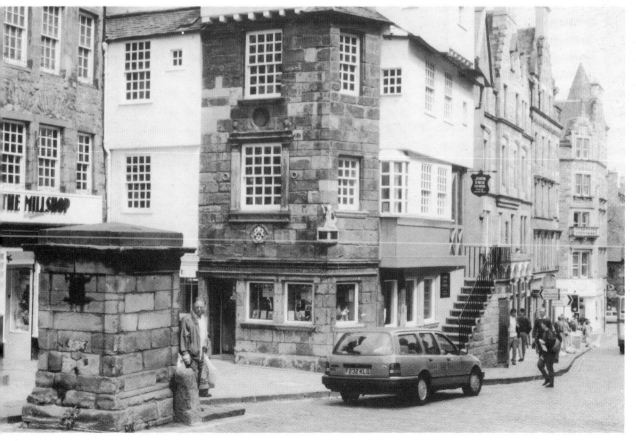

ROYAL INFIRMARY, LAURISTON PLACE

The foundation stone of the new building to replace the inadequate Infirmary Street premises was laid by the Prince of Wales in October 1870 and opened nine years later at a cost of £300,000, most of which was raised by public subscription. Imposing a Bryce's design is when seen from Heriot's lawn, curative medicine was still in its infancy, and doctors were sadly limited in their power to do much good. We are more fortunate today. What is striking, apart from the growth of the trees, is how much better the lawn is kept than in the late nineteenth century.

AUL F882

HERIOT'S MOSPITAL, EDINBURGH, 19 C.W.W.

HERIOT'S SCHOOL

The exterior of this fine building is little changed from when it was completed in the seventeenth century but inside the amenities and the curriculum have altered out of all recognition. In George Washington Wilson's day there were 120 boarders and 90 day boys but none was available and so his assistant was told to recline beside the flower bed! Some of the Heriot money was used in the nineteenth century to fund free schools in poor areas of Edinburgh and the Watt Institution and School of Arts which later became the Heriot-Watt University also benefitted. Amongst its staff in the mid 1880s was a Mr Whaley Nutt, lecturer in elocution whose name must have proved a stimulus to student humour if not articulation.

THE ROYAL MILE

Looking down the High Street towards Canongate Tolbooth, the late nineteenth century view is a curious mixture of bustle and decay. There are plenty of people about, a few casually standing in the middle of the road. Some shops are doing well, like the hosiers and hatters at number 172. Look at the piles of elegant felt hats wrapped up in paper and hanging up outside. But there are also shops boarded up, for sale or to let as are some of the flats in this heavily populated area. Redevelopment in the 1950's and 1960's has undoubtedly cleaned up the Canongate. The pawnbrokers and the second-hand clothes shops have gone, and the whole environment is much tidier thanks to cleaned stonework and litter bins carefully placed.

AUL B576

THE CANONGATE TOLBOOTH

A woman pokes her head out of the window of her third floor room and some pedestrians pause to watch Wilson at work on this misty morning. The Tolbooth was no mere museum then as it has become since. In the 1870's it housed the police, the fire brigade's engine, the inspector of the poor and the Canongate's Literary Society's reading and news rooms. Seats outside the Tolbooth have replaced the steps of the cross as a resting place and the clock face shows the date of its last renovation, 1884. The Ballad store is long gone as is the Midlothian Loan Office, one of the thirty-six city pawnbrokers in the 1870's.

HOLYROOD PALACE

The Palace and Abbey were on every tourist's itinerary particularly the room in Queen Mary's Apartments where the unfortunate Rizzio was murdered. Queen Victoria and her family restored the royal connection by annually spending two nights there en route to Balmoral, to the great enthusiasm of the local population, but the Palace was not much loved. The problem for a long time was the location on low marshy ground, and the nearby "dingy and malodorous" Canongate. Efforts were made in the 1840's to drain the ground, smooth it level and clear some of the clutter of old houses roundabout, but the arrival of the railway offset this improvement to some extent.

The Palace looks fine in Wilson's 1865 view, and Royal Terrace stands out proudly beyond. The twentieth century has seen little change on the near side of the Place but Abbeymount and Montrose Terrace have altered and the skyline towards the north is very different. The air of Edinburgh is much cleaner than in Wilson's day now there are no longer thousands of coal fires.

HOLYROOD PARK TOWARDS THE CALTON HILL

A gentleman out for a walk pauses to allow Wilson to include him in this study looking towards the Palace over Haggis Knowe. His collie is eyeing up the sheep. The great 240 foot chimney of the Edinburgh Gas Works belches out smoke but the Calton Jail and Royal High School are just visible. The newly formed road up to the rifle ranges at Hunter's Bog is very obvious. The demolition of chimneys and general decline in the use of coal combine to enable Brian Kiloh to provide a much sharper photograph of the east end of Princes Street, but as elsewhere the trees conceal important features such as the Abbey window. Archery was the traditional sport practised here, but a bowling green has arrived close to the Boundary Wall, it being a sport gaining popularity everywhere in late nineteenth century Scotland.

ARTHUR'S SEAT FROM ST LEONARD'S

The Commonwealth Swimming Pool and the Pollock Halls of Residence surround St Leonard's House, erected in 1870 by the publisher Thomas Nelson for his eldest son, to keep his residence within sight of the family works at Parkside.

HOLYROOD PALACE FROM REGENT TERRACE GARDENS

t is just possible that the pile of dressed and numbered stones may have been from the historic Trinity Church, taken down by the North British Railway Company when it built its line through to Waverley in 1848. There is a clear view of the Abbey and Palace; the imposing fountain was erected in 1859 as part of a process instigated by Prince Albert of tidying up the forecourt. Beyond are Salisbury Crags and the walks so much loved by generations of Edinburgh residents, none more than Sir Walter Scott who resorted there morning and evening whenever "engaged with a favourite author or new subject of study". One suspects the Labrador dog would much rather be there than in the Regent Terrace Gardens where only the hedges run riot.

BURNS' MONUMENT AND SALISBURY CRAGS

Few people can have created more employment for the Scottish monument and statue business than Burns. Edinburgh's was finished in 1830 and contained a statue by Flaxman. There was also a small museum, admission 6d. The marble statue of Burns was subsequently moved to the University and finally to the National Gallery. It was ridiculed by some for depicting Burns as a Roman senator rather than a rude ploughman addressing a daisy. Behind the monument are the close-packed houses of the Canongate, and the Holyrood Brewery chimney indicates a moderate east wind. The Crags stand out well. Much of the older property was subsequently swept away or renovated as is evident from the present day study, which shows the Canongate to be very much improved.

ROYAL HIGH SCHOOL

This fine Grecian building, reckoned by some to be the finest of its kind in Edinburgh was completed in 1829, and there the Royal High School remained until its removal to East Barnton. Regent Road was then adapted for use by the projected Scottish Assembly but the referendum of 1978 put an end to that idea for the time being. In the nineteenth century, the Royal High School diversified its curriculum away from the original concentration on classics to offer scientific and commercial subjects: the versatile John Thompson in 1893 was teaching Shorthand Writing and Hindustani. Wilson's photograph c 1866 is interesting also because it shows his photographic tent and a panier for the glass plates behind the railings of the Burns' Monument. The early Victorian photographer was encumbered with equipment, and George Washington Wilson needed assistance. At least three helpers appear to be on hand. He later switched from using a tent to working from a specially equipped mobile studio.

Wilson's Photographic Van parked at the kerb in Princes Street.

CALTON HILL

In a city not short of vantage points, the Calton Hill was much loved by visitors and photographers alike. Black's **Guide to Scotland** (1882 edition) said that "the views presented from various points are striking and extensive", and George Washington Wilson was often up here. The camera looks out past the memorial to the distinguished Scots philosopher Dugald Stewart towards Leith Street and St James Square. The gun, a Russian trophy from the Crimean War, is aligned roughly in the direction of the Melville Monument in St Andrews Square which stands up above the clutter of chimneys and housing. As well as the banks and the institutions, there was considerable private housing in this area, some of it of no great standard.

The railings were taken away during the Second World War and the Calton site loses by that. To the right the St James Centre (1965-70) rises in what some regard as an unsympathetic intrusion, but this is still a fine view urban view. The replacement cannon now points towards Princes Street, where the North British Hotel stands guard. And whereas Wilson had to carry not just his camera and a tripod but also glass plates and chemicals, the modern photographer travels more lightly.

LEITH FROM CALTON HILL

The immediate vicinity of the Calton Hill included some elegant New Town terraces — Leopold Place and Windsor Street — but the more one looks towards Leith, the more obscured the view becomes by smoke from the many works in the Leith area. Leith was always more industrial than Edinburgh, with flour mills, paintworks, roperies, tanneries and breweries, but even so, a few masts in the harbour can be glimpsed through the smog. Leith Walk is clearly visible, as is the North British Railway Company's Leith Central Station opened in 1869, which was the terminus of through trains from Glasgow and the west as well as of suburban services. The Caledonian Railway had its station at North Leith. Neither proved very successful in coping with the competition of trams and buses, and by the early 1960's passenger services to Leith had gone. So, also, alas, had Leith's municipal independence won from Edinburgh in 1833, and much of the industry, though the huge SAI factory and Chancelot Mills ensure that the skyline is not indisputably controlled by residential tower blocks. Cranes have bred successfully in the harbour area, and in the distance is Inchkeith guarding Leith Roads as it has always done.

CALTON HILL TOWARDS GRANTON

It is staggering to think how many people lived in the massive tenements of Victorian Greenside, set cheek by jowl with the elega[nt] terraces of London Road and Leopold Place, and there would have been more than enough to fill Lady Glenorchy's Free Chur[ch] several times over, had they wished to attend. Only the castellated front now remains, and most of the tenements to the west ha[ve] gone, sacrificed to make a massive roundabout. While St Mary's Bellevue remains in use as a place of worship, the Albany Stre[et] Free Church and spire have gone.

CALTON HILL TO PRINCES STREET

George Washington Wilson loved this particular viewpoint; "from here", he wrote "Princes Street with its ceaseless travellers and countless buildings is seen to best advantage". Most of the distinctive landmarks of the city are visible: the Scott Monument, the Castle and St Giles. In our first view, the North Bridge has scaffolding on it, which along with the tracks in Princes Street for the horse drawn trams, suggests a date of c1876. The second, taken by the photographer Alexander Inglis and registered by George Washington Wilson & Co. in June 1905, shows the North British Hotel dominating the east end of Princes Street as if it had always been there. Otherwise much is as it was thirty years previously except for the remodeled North Bridge. Rising out of the Low Calton burial ground is the Obelisk to five Political Reformers who were transported to Australia in 1793: few nowadays could name any of them or their cause. In the foreground is the impressive Edinburgh Prison, which ill-briefed travellers were liable to mistake for the Castle. The west-most section, with imposing gatehouse, was the jail. Next to it came the Town and County Bridewell, or house of correction, and to the east was a Debtor's Jail. The Calton Gaol was swept away in the 1930's to make way for New St Andrew House, a building which time has not served well. It, like the obelisk, is in dire need of a complete face-lift, something which the North British Hotel is in process of acquiring. The trams have gone, and in their place the ubiquitous car, and less ubiquitous but clog Princes Street.

CALTON HILL ACROSS TO THE OLD TOWN

The current landscape is shaped by St Andrew's House and its frontage. If it is indeed the most impressive work of architecture in Scotland during the inter-war years, then we can only be thankful that there was not more. The figures capping the columns represent Architecture, Statecraft, Health, Agriculture, Fisheries and Education. Waverley Station was being enlarged yet again in Wilson's photograph but the North Bridge remains unwidened which suggests a date of c1880. The governor's house which is all that remains of the Calton Jail, has a well-kept garden and magnificent location.

CALTON JAIL FROM WAVERLEY STATION

The Calton Hill buildings, Governor's house and Calton Jail look over Waverley Station in this classic and familiar Victorian study. The Station platforms are unsheltered at this east end, and the masses of rolling stock indicate the pressure Waverley was under. This eventually led to a radical programme of improvement in the 1890's making it the largest station in terms of platform accommodation anywhere in Britain after Waterloo. Cleaners are at work on the rolling stock and on the platform by the water tower a lone woman sorts through masses of NB laundry.

There had been at one time a temporary goods shed in front of the cork manufacturer's business, and a laden cart laden with barrels for the Holyrood breweries is about to start, but so great was passenger traffic at Waverley Station that the goods work was moved away. The railway is now less busy, but decades of vibration have taken their toll and southern slopes require stabilization with nets.

CALTON HILL

The tombstones of the Old Calton Burying Ground stand up clearly while other memorials are set in the wall of the Gaol. To the l
is the Rock Photographic studio, which provided stiff competition to G. W. Wilson & Co. The primary focus of this photograph is t
Calton Hill and its buildings; from left to right, the Observatory and Observatory House, Dugald Stewart's Monument, Edinburgl
disgrace (the unfinished National Monument) and the Nelson Monument, intended to signal the time both to the Old Town and
ships in the Firth of Forth. The last called forth from William McGonagall a few lines of verse which are bad even by his standarc
(**Poetic Gems** 1890)

> "Then as for Nelson's Monument that stands on the Calton Hill,
> As the tourist gazes thereon, with wonder his heart does fill
> As he thinks on Admiral Nelson who did the Frenchmen kill"

Our modern study looks up towards the Calton Hill, but from beside the freed slave of the Emancipation Monument erected in 18
to commemorate the many soldiers of Scottish descent who fought on the Union side in the American Civil War. Abraham Lincoln
figure tops this remarkable monument.

THE CITY OBSERVATORIES

Despite being equipped in 1889 with a superb telescope from Dunecht House in Aberdeenshire, the gift of the Earl of Crawford, the city observatories had been long working in increasingly difficult conditions. The vibration of the trains below threw the astronomers' observations out, and it was with relief that they moved in 1893 to the new observatory on Blackford Hill, a much more peaceful location.

REGISTER HOUSE

The Iron Duke in bronze by Steell faces out from Register House as he has done ever since 1852. Wellington apparently thought the likeness of himself remarkable enough for him to order two copies cast for Apley House and Eton. Generations of historians and lawyers have worked in Register House on the records of Scotland, with increasing comfort but also of late much tighter security. The frontage appears unchanged until one looks very closely: the staircase, for instance, has been remodeled and the elegant gas lamps are gone. The private Edinburgh Gas Company's head office was just along the road in Waterloo Place. The security box now houses a barometer.

THE GENERAL POST OFFICE

The laying of the foundation stone of the GPO in Edinburgh on the 23rd September 1861 was Prince Albert's last official duty before his sudden death from typhoid on December 14th. He suggested the urns on the ballustrade which have since vanished. George Washington Wilson's view is taken not long after the opening of the building in 1866. The tramways began to be laid from 1871 onwards. The traffic in those days managed to flow without traffic lights.

The GPO offered a remarkable service in Victorian times. It was open from 7 am to 10 pm, and there were 7 deliveries in the Edinburgh area, starting at 7 am and finishing at 7.30 pm.

HORSE TRAM WITH PASSENGERS DISEMBARKING

CRANSTON & ELLIOT

HOUSE FURNISHERS

CABINETMAKERS & UPHOLSTERERS

CRANSTON & ELLIOT FAMILY DRAPERS COSTURIERS & SILK MERCERS

CRANSTON & ELLIOT FAMILY DRAPERS & UPHOLSTERERS

G.W.WILSON & CO. ABERDEEN.   LORD HIGH COMMISSIONERS PROCESSION, EDINBURGH — MAY, 1884

NORTH BRIDGE

The Victorians loved a procession of any kind. Here a large crowd has turned out to watch the carriages of the High Commissioner to the General Assembly and his entourage en route from Holyrood Palace to St Giles for the opening service. It is striking how well turned out in suits and hats, are all the spectators and how thickly they are massed outside Register House and on the Bridge. The cramped conditions forced a re-design of the North Bridge in the 1890's, and improvement is very evident today. On the east side of the present bridge is the King's Own Scottish Borderers Boer War memorial, put there in 1906. The renovation of the North British Hotel to cost £20 million, it is said, is clearly well in progress. Gone are Cranston & Elliot, the Victorian drapers who claimed to have "the largest and cheapest dress stock in the city" Curiously, their advertising tended to feature not their building but the adjacent New Post Office!

71

SOUTH BRIDGE

The Old Quad of the University of Edinburgh has changed very little in appearance since George Washington Wilson took this picture in the early 1860's, save for the addition of the dome in 1879. A Victorian student would hate the loss of the railings and the street lamps, but be re-assured to find across the road the familiar James Thin's bookshop outside which a coachman waits. There's not much evidence of any students about. In George Washington Wilson's time medicine was by far the most important discipline, turning out more graduates than all the others put together.

AUL C0643

SURGEONS' HALL

the distance, over the Old Quad is the gilded statue of "Youth bearing the torch of learning" placed in 1879 to top out the new ome. In the foreground, a messenger boy takes a rest against a helpful lamp post, and a trail of droppings mark the passage of e horse trams, to the irritation doubtless of the lady with the long skirts sweeping across the road. But the modern scene is not eaner. Look at the litter in and around the gutter, and the profusion of shop signs and street instructions. Surgeons' Hall offered a nge of teaching in medicine with in the 1890's Dr Sophia Jex-Blake not just breaching the male monopoly of lecturing but acting Dean of the School.

PRINCES STREET LOOKING EAST

This upper balcony in Princes Street opposite the Scott Monument was a favourite vantage point of George Washington Wilson and he returned to it several times to take a series of views from 1859 onwards which excited contemporary attention for their clarity and ability to catch people in motion. In this photograph from 1863, what is noticeable is how everyone has their head covered, gentlemen with toppers, ladies mostly with parasols as they promenade along. There appears to be no Highway Code in operation, to judge from the trap proceeding down the middle of Princes Street. Notice the American flag flying above no 31 where a shipping agent for the Allan, Cunard and White Star companies had his office.

Brian Kiloh has been driven to a slightly different vantage point, but his view underlines the firmness of current road discipline. The Waverley Market started life with the North British Railway Company as a vegetable market but was handed over in March 1869 to the City which proceeded to build an ornamental garden at the Princes Street level, the hall underneath being used for various purposes such as the funfair in the 1950's. Very dilapidated by then, it was demolished and has been rebuilt in the last few years to form a new Waverley Market.

AUL C3322xa

PRINCES STREET LOOKING WEST

A horse coach waits to collect passengers for a trip to the Forth Bridge. The round trip cost 1/6d and the service continued lo
after the completion of the Bridge, so great was fascination with it. The cab rank is doing more business, but the Waverley Gard
is almost deserted save for one or two spectators leaning over the railings on the Station side. Shrubs and pots of flowers are set c
in meticulous order: our taste today is for a less regimented effect. The gardens can still boast wonderful displays.

WAVERLEY STATION

The original Waverley Station was really three stations; the North British serving the south, the Edinburgh and Glasgow to the west and the Edinburgh, Perth and Dundee for the north, the terminus buildings of which were at right angles to the other two. To travel to the north, the line first ran under Princes Street in a tunnel issuing at Scotland Street, thence to Granton where passengers transferred to a ferry acoss the Forth and so on. It might be interesting to re-open the disused tunnel under Princes Street, which has long been abandoned by the railways and mushroom growers alike. Behind Waverley and Market Street rises the Old Town. Apart from the alterations to the station, the roof of which needs attention, it is Market Street and the North Bridge buildings that have undergone the most change: the Scotsman and Evening News Offices on the north-west corner, and the Carlton Hotel across the way. The whole site was comprehensively redeveloped in the late 1890's and the Scotsman proprietors got their stance for a mere £120,000. What would it fetch today?

PRINCES STREET GARDENS TO THE OLD TOWN

George Washington Wilson visited this spot several times. The earliest view (c1863) shows the old Waverley Bridge whic replaced a roadway known as little Mound. At the tunnel mouth is the primitive semaphore signalling system, and some of th uncomfortable rolling stock of the Edinburgh and Glasgow. Philp's Commercial Hotel (The Cockburn) at the far side was used b Thomas Cook as headquarters for his Scottish tours and proudly advertised that it had pianos in all the parlours and saloons a well as Turkish Baths in the basement. The second view c1885 shows the replacement Waverley Bridge of the early 1870's whic did away with the tunnels and pushed out the platforms. Trees and roofs alike blanket the station today, though the side panels ar visible of the third Waverley Station bridge finished in 1876. The City Chambers was extended in 1901-4 to push out massively int Cockburn Street.

SCOTT MONUMENT FROM ST DAVID STREET c1865

Of the eventual sixty four statues depicting characters in his work intended for this shrine to Sir Walter Scott relatively few are in place at the time of this photograph as the bare plinths indicate. Yet the Monument dominates the area — it is fortunate that the initial notion to site it in Charlotte Square Gardens was abandoned well before the architect Kemp's untimely drowning in the Union Canal in 1844. Quite why Sir Walter looks towards the New rather than towards the Old Town is open to challenge. Behind him the head office of the Bank of Scotland is being rebuilt but the bottom end of the new Cockburn Street is complete. Several of the businesses in St David Street have a familiar Edinburgh ring to them. On the west side is A. Dott, Carver, Gilder and Picture Framer, and at the corner is Kennington and Jenner, the drapers and mercers. After a major fire in 1892, Jenners was given a massive and magnificent new department store completed in 1895. Less attractive are the replacement buildings on the east side, the Scottish Provident and Ivanhoe house of the 1960's. Gone is the horse and cart, the saddler and harness maker (R. Spaven) at number 654, the cobbles and gas lamps. And taller buildings reduce the earlier power of the Scott Monument.

LIVINGSTONE STATUE, EAST PRINCES STREET GARDENS

David Livingstone was one of the great figures of the Victorian world. The famous missionary and explorer received the freedom of the city in September 1857, as did his discoverer, Dr Stanley in June 1890 after a previous triumphal reception in 1872. The statue is somewhat dwarfed by the Scott Monument, but has an appropriate garland. Just in front of the Monument railings is George Washington Wilson's photographic tent, and a panier of plates beside the gentleman watching proceedings from the bench.

There are more benches now, but much less knowledge of Livingstone and his work. One conundrum is apparent, that the style of the inscription "Livingstone", has been altered at some time. The statue, by Mrs D. O. Hill, widow of the famous pioneer of photography, was unveiled by Lord Provost Falshaw on the 15th of September, 1876 — three years after Livingstone's death in Africa.

PRINCES STREET LOOKING EAST

This early view by George Washington Wilson of the Scott Monument was taken c1860 from Hanover Street and catches a street busy with motion, especially towards the far end where the markets and cab ranks coincided. On the right looms the gas company's chimney and to the left on the corner of Hanover Street is the United Kingdom Telegraph Company's Office, a very recent arrival. The telephone was to follow somewhat later, the first being introduced to Edinburgh in 1880. Notice the pile of horsedung awaiting collection, and the full length of dresses and cloaks. A hundred years later the frontages are very different but the traffic just as busy.

PRINCES STREET GARDENS TO THE BANK OF SCOTLAND

Victorian Edinburgh was the centre of safe and successful banking in contrast, it has to be said, to Glasgow which had more tha
one catastrophic failure. None of the banks, which did not stint themselves when it came to building, had a more impressive hea
office than the Bank of Scotland, with its superb position. To the right is New College, and below awaiting instruction is one of th
North British's crack express locomotives, the Glasgow, brought into service in 1876 for the main line to Glasgow. It is still a fin
view today even if the chances of seeing a steam engine are all too slight. In the background the Braid Hills and the Pentlands ar
visible.

SCOTT MONUMENT FROM PRINCES STREET GARDENS

Access to these Gardens was at the discretion of the Princes Street proprietors until 1876 when the City took over responsibility. Scythesmen are hard at work on the slopes; they have a long day ahead of them. The Royal Hotel was one of the oldest established hotels in Princes Street. Donald MacGregor, who took it over in 1864, lost no time in putting his name up and claiming to have the best views of the Gardens, Castle and Arthur's Seat. There was clearly stiff competition which was on occasion cut throat: MacGregor warned visitors to be careful that Cabmen and Porters did not take them elsewhere "as it has caused parties great annoyance". The Gardens are surprisingly under appreciated today, except by office workers at lunchtime.

PRINCES STREET, EDINBURGH, FROM SCOTT MONUMENT, LOOKING W.   11,024   G.W.W.

SCOTT MONUMENT TO PRINCES STREET, LOOKING WEST

A fine sweep along Princes Street towards Hanover Street and the Royal Institution. What a variety of businesses were to be foun
there in Victorian times: a famous gunsmith, John Dickson, the tartan and tweed manufacturers, Romanes and Patterson, and o
the corner of Hanover Street, Thornton & Co who specialised in waterproofs, knapsacks, belting, trousers, capes, life-jacket
covers for horses — the list is endless. Just by the Mound letter box is a board put out by one of Wilson's competitors, James Howi
the photographer whose studio was at number 60b, advertising rival views of Scotland. The statue of Queen Victoria, flattering
slim, still presides over the scene from the Royal Scottish Academy which was formerly the Royal Institution but most of the prese
day shops are part of national chains, rather than peculiar to Edinburgh. There's no doubt about their popularity! The Caledoni
Hotel and St Mary's Cathedral complete this modern day view, still one of the finest in Europe.

WILSON STATUE, PRINCES STREET GARDENS AT FOOT OF MOUNT 1865

John Wilson's statue must be seen every day by thousands of people but very few, one suspects, could say much about him. He wa
Professor of Moral Philosophy at the University of Edinburgh, a job for which he seems to have been particularly ill-qualified excep
in terms of his politics. His real distinction was as a writer for Blackwoods Magazine under the pseudonym of 'Christopher North
Hence the quill in the hand of the statue raised by his friends after his death in 1854. It took them some time to raise the necessar
funds for this bronze likeness, said to be a very good one, and the statue was only unveiled in March 1865. A group of ladies sit c
the lowest step of the base; it is to be hoped they knew whose the statue was, because no inscription has yet been added! Th
modern setting is overshadowed by trees and a hot dog stand adds nothing to the dignity of his situation.

FOOT OF THE MOUND

In contrast to Wilson's solitary horse tram waiting for business, the Faith Mission hold an outreach service. What's more, they allc
a woman to preach, although one or two of the men look as if it's their turn next. It is not an easy task and never has been. Nineteen
century Edinburgh was not short of evangelistic endeavour. There were dozens of city missionaries, including missionaries f
'special' classes; for the cabmen, the police, sufferers from intemperance, Irish Roman Catholics and Free Church Highlande
Why were cabmen seen as particularly unregenerate? Because they worked on Sundays, perhaps?

THE ROYAL SCOTTISH ACADEMY FROM HANOVER STREET

This building, the Royal Institution, was originally shared by a number of bodies; the Royal Society, the Scottish Society for Painting, the Royal Institution for the Encouragement of Fine Arts, and the Board of Trustees for Fisheries and Manufacturers, who had a textile drawing and design school. Wilson knew this place well, and this is a superb photograph, aided by his ability to set up his tripod in the middle of the road without undue interference, a privilege given to no modern photographer. Note on the left 'fresh strawberries' available rather than pizza and the elegant awning to Yerbury's shop.

ROYAL SCOTTISH ACADEMY TO PRINCES STREET

he camera attracts attention both from the Mound policeman and a girl who unwisely pauses on the crossing. There was no reen man' in those days nor any pavement artistry to attract the attention of passers by. The trees lining the pavement walk have een joined by an avenue of flags, but there is little left hereabouts at any level of the Victorian frontage on the north side. The New ub, for instance replaced their distinctive 1834 premises in 1966 with a much more modern affair including a swimming pool. By lan Ramsay's statue is the much loved Floral Clock, a welcome addition to the City's attractions.

107-108 PRINCES STREET

Here is a challenge to spot the external changes. The upper lines of the former Liberal Club between Frederick and Castle Stre
remain much as before. It was formerly the Palace Hotel of 1867 and taken over by the Liberals in 1890 to keep up with Scotti:
Conservatives whose club was a few doors along at no 112. The ornamental ironwork on the roof has gone, as have the flagpo
and the urns. Mackies the Bakers of Edinburgh Rock fame have been lost since the Second World War, and their insignia of pate
— purveyors to the Queen and H.R.H. The Prince of Wales — are doubtless no more. Also a casualty of time is Taylor's showroor
Primarily an upholsterer and cabinetmaker, the firm combined their activities with funeral undertaking, the manufacture of blinc
and a house-letting agency — an interesting combination of roles!

GEORGE STREET, LOOKING EAST

11.40 am on a quite sunny day in George Street which has always tended to play second fiddle to Princes Street. This was home ground for Insurance Companies (the Standard Life, the Royal Fire, the Caledonian and the Phoenix), and next to the Clydesdale Bank on the corner of Frederick Street was Patterson's the music sellers. Generations of bus and lorry drivers have cursed the George Street statues. The George IVth statue was disliked by the Victorian authorities, one of whom suggested that the pose could be sustained only if the monarch had a kangaroo's tail concealed in his robes!

GEORGE STREET, LOOKING WEST

he north side of George Street was at this time c1865 an interesting mixture of residential and business housing. Behind Pitt's
tatue is a chemist, an undertaker and a stationer's and along the street are quite a number of awnings, not that there seem to be
ny customers about, which allows an apron-clad assistant to sit out on the steps of the plinth. Building societies have moved in to
olonize George Street, but there are still plenty of familiar activities such as the auction rooms.

CHARLOTTE SQUARE GARDENS

Tucked away in these private gardens, and largely ignored, is Edinburgh's Albert Memorial, a statue depicting the Prince Consort surrounded by figures from every walk of life — the Services, Nobility, Labour and Science. Unveiled on the 17th of August 1876 Wilson may have been present in person at the ceremony. He had, after all, known Albert quite well at Balmoral. From the freshness of the gravel and the staging timber in the background, the photograph was certainly taken shortly before or after the formal proceedings.

GEORGE STREET AND THE NORTHERN NEW TOWN

Across the roofs of Princes and George Street to Fettes and in the distance the Bridges, you can see how much Edinburgh is a attractive mixture of housing and park. This is curiously one view that George Washington Wilson never took.

WEST PRINCES STREET GARDENS

No Victorian Park would have been complete without a bandstand. Princes Street Gardens received a military band concert twice a week during the summer — doubtless lots of Sullivan — and special programmes from some of the many local bands. The Ross bandstand still hosts innumerable events. Nearby Charlotte Chapel Baptist Church used to hold outdoor services there but the original bandstand is now relegated to the useful role of a shelter beside a children's play area.

ROSS FOUNTAIN

This ornate fountain in West Princes Street Gardens was purchased from France where it had been a feature of an International Exhibition by an Edinburgh gunsmith, Mr Ross of Napier Road who gifted it in 1869 to the Gardens. It arrived from the Continent in a kit of 122 pieces but was put together successfully and one hundred and twenty years later flows just as attractively.

A GROUP OF VICTORIAN CHILDREN AT PLAY BESIDE THE FOUNTAIN.

ST JOHN'S CHURCH

This normally very busy junction is almost deserted at 3.45 pm, apart from one horse tram, which suggests it's a Sunday. To the right Clark & Crawford offer sherry, claret and the finest whisky at 30/- a gallon. On the other side is the Osborne Hotel destroyed by fire in 1879 and rebuilt as a club, then torn down in 1935 to make way for a store. The Binn's clock has always been a favourite meeting place. Across the road is the red sandstone Caledonian Hotel (1903), that railway company's response to the North British at the other end of Princes Street. The Hotel has outlived the Caley Station which closed in 1965.

Miss Catherine Sinclair's Fountain. Donated in 1859 by the daughter of the agricultural writer Sir John Sinclair, this was a much-used watering point for carters. Horses and fountains alike have been swept away. Miss Sinclair, authoress of **Modern Accomplishments**, paid for fountains and public benches in many parts of the city: do any survive?

LOTHIAN ROAD

This very early view is alas damaged but it does give an idea of how Lothian Road looked in 1859. Notice the wall rather tha railings to St Cuthbert's graveyard, the absence of the Sinclair fountain, and the works in progress on the left hand side in tl Caledonian Station. One of the placards advertises a "Working Men's Flower Show: A Celebration of Plants". No bus shelters those days.

ST CUTHBERT'S GRAVEYARD

St John's Episcopal Church appears to lack stained glass for most of the windows to the south. St Cuthbert's graveyard contains hundreds of stones, monuments and enclosures, and an interesting present day challenge is to locate where some of the Victorian markers have been moved. The figure memorial to the Rev David Dickson DD, is still in place to the right, but others are gone, defaced or broken.

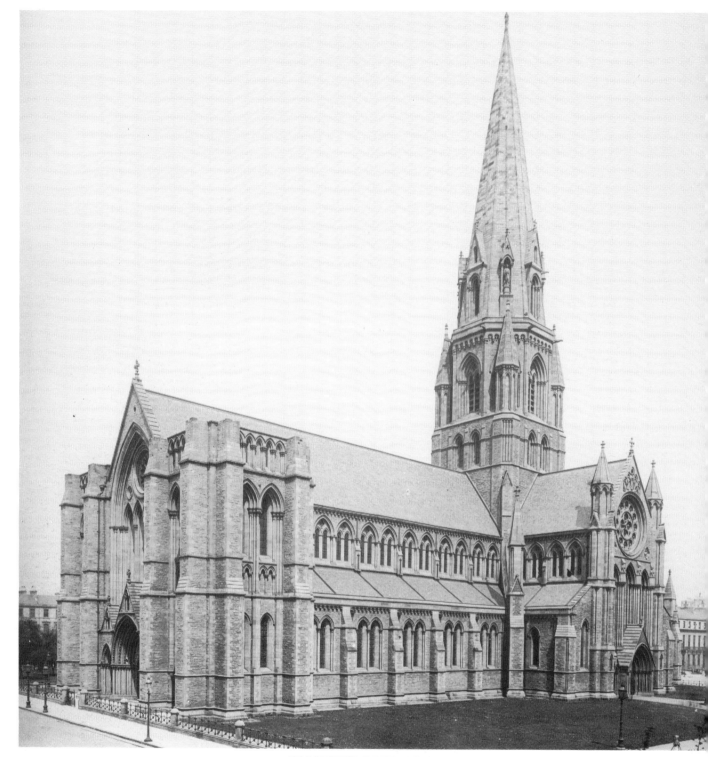

ST MARY'S CATHEDRAL

In 1871 the Episcopalian church was bequeathed the substantial sum of £100,000 from the estate of the Misses Walker who owned the lands of Coates which comprised a fair chunk of the West End, the money to be used to erect a cathedral. An architect was quickly appointed, Sir Gilbert Scott, and the foundation stone laid by the Duke of Buccleuch on the 21st of May 1874. The church was consecrated for use and opened in October 1879 despite the fact that as the money was exhausted, the western spires were only complete to the height of the nave. Scott's sons finished the spires in 1917. Contemporaries were agreed that the Cathedral was one of the most important additions to the ecclesiastical architecture of Britain, and certainly the skyline of the West End is shaped by its three spires. The Palmerstone Place doorway, through which Victorian worshippers passed for the Sunday services (11, 3.30 and 7) was particularly admired, its red granite harmonizing well with the Stirlingshire stone of the exterior.

DEAN BRIDGE

Telford's magnificent bridge was built between 1829 and 1831 to enable Provost Learmonth who paid for its construction develop the estate of Dean. Below this 100 foot high bridge lay the community of Dean Village with its flourmills and tannery, the last a somewhat smelly business which closed only in the 1960's. The mill wheels no longer turn and the lade across the Water Leith is merely scenic, but the river is much cleaner now than in its Victorian heyday when it was both a source of power and drain. Overlooking the bridge is Randolph Cliff which guards the south end of Randolph Crescent. The bridge parapet had to heightened in 1912 because of its attraction for suicides.

BELGRAVE CRESCENT

The elegance of this crescent is well caught by George Washington Wilson in this view (unfortunately damaged to the right) acros[s] the Dean Village. The gardens in front were laid right out in 1876 but the trees in them have now reached such height and profusio[n] as to conceal the crescent entirely. Only Holy Trinity is now visible. Opened in 1838 as an Episcopal Church, it has had an up an[d] down career. Statistics show it to have had a small but wealthy congregation in 1853 of about 200. Later decline and rising fabri[c] costs led to its sale in 1957 to the South of Scotland Electricity Board who converted it for use as an electricity transformer station. [It] has just, however, been bought back in 1989 for reconversion to Christian use.

CRAIG LOCKHART HYDROPATHIC ESTAB^T EDINBURGH 8324 G.W.W.

CRAIGLOCKHART HYDROPATHIC

This private health hotel for the rich was opened in 1880 and had the usual facilities common to such establishments; a swimming pool, billiard table, medical facilities and lots of servants and also — or so it claimed — the finest croquet lawn in Scotland. It offered to its clientele tours and excursions to the City and surrounding countryside. Never very successful, it became a recuperative hospital during the First World War and amongst its residents were Wilfred Owen and Siegfreid Sassoon. It became a convent school in 1920 and acquired a chapel in 1933. It has since passed from Craiglockhart College of Education to become part of Napier Polytechnic of Edinburgh.

CRAIGLEITH QUARRY

Quite a lot of the stone used in nineteenth century Edinburgh came from this quarry and from its sister quarries at Blackhall and Barnton. Craigleith stone was used, for example, for the National Monument, the University Old Quad and Leith Town Hall. But it was clearly reaching exhaustion by the time this view was taken, and the bottom was being allowed to fill with water. Bungalows now march over the fields of Comely Bank farm and though Daniel Stewart's holds its own, an office block entirely masks the Castle.

EDINBURGH FROM CRAIGLEITH QUARRY. 2362. G.W.W

ROCKVILLE, MERCHISTON

Some of us remember this extraordinary house which was demolished in 1965, the victim of neglect and dry rot. It was the creation of James Gowans in 1858, later knighted, who had as you can see some very distinct ideas of his own as to design. Even the wrought-iron railings were peculiar, being a grid composition with his initials worked in. Some sense of his style can still be gained from Lammerburn on the other side of Napier Road or the Redhall quarrymen's cottages off Lanark Road. What sticks in the memory is the mosaic of stones. Even the fragment of the wall left today is worth a look.

BLACKFORD HILL

The Commonwealth Pool and the Pollock Halls of Residence stand out in front of Arthur's Seat but the most striking difference over the hundred years since Wilson took his photograph is the way in which housing has spread to cover the fields which even in George Washington Wilson's day were under threat. In 1884, the same year as Blackford Hill was acquired as a public park, the Edinburgh suburban railway was completed. It used to carry a passenger service which ceased in September 1962. There is talk however, of reviving the 'sub' and re-opening Morningside, Newington and other stations.

ST LEONARD'S HILL

ollowers of Sir Walter Scott's **Heart of Midlothian** were encouraged to identify this as Jeannie and David Dean's cottage, and the ssociation was still sufficiently strong to make it worthwhile for Louis Wilson to take this photograph in 1902. Behind is the St eonard's Carriage Works, one of the twenty-five such builders in Edinburgh, soon to be faced with extinction by the motor car rms. Works and cottage are now alike gone.

DUDDINGSTON LOCH

Few Victorian tourists who stayed for any length of time in Edinburgh can have failed to take a turn through Holyrood Park. The cab fare for the 2½ mile circuit called Queen's Drive was 3/- an hour, allowing for time to sightsee or to climb. Samson's Ribs and the Windy Goule were on the route and from the latter we look down on the Loch and Duddingston Village and beyond to Joppa on the left and the Lammermuirs in the far distance. The St Leonards branch of the Edinburgh and Dalkeith is almost completely concealed. It lasted until 1968 and an occasional treat was to watch the Holyrood sheep being gathered for a special train perhaps to Gorgie Mart. Craigmillar Estate fills the farmland to the south and also to be seen is Prestonfield Golf course. The Loch area is almost entirely unspoiled and unchanged.

SWANS ON DUDDINGSTON LOCH

The Loch has always played home to a wide range of birds, some resident and other migratory but only comparatively recently has been designated as a bird sanctuary. These swans have never been in danger but the duck and the geese would have tempted Victorian wildfowlers.

CRAIGMILLAR CASTLE

Another popular outing was to Craigmillar Castle which could be reached either by tram or from Duddingston station. An histori ruin, more or less roofless, it was just what the Victorians loved with its links to Mary Queen of Scots. Was it not to Craigmillar th she retreated after the murder of Rizzio in 1566 and where the plot was hatched to get rid of her husband Darnley? Georg Washington Wilson visited Craigmillar several times and as was his invariable practice uses his assistant to add some huma interest to the scene.

ROSLIN

Probably the most popular Victorian outing was to Roslin. It held many attractions; strawberries in the village, a romantic glen, mouldering ruin in Roslin Castle and the medieval Chapel. Excursionists could chose to travel to either Roslin station on the Penecuik line or Rosinlee Station on the Peebes line, neither of which was very close. A cheaper option was to go by coach from the Waverley steps and also take in Hawthornden and Dalkeith Palace. Great efforts have recently been made to landscape the glen, restore its beautiful walks and bring it back to the scenic charm of George Washington Wilson's day.

ROSLIN CHAPEL

he Chapel was and is Episcopalian Church of Scotland. Services in Victorian times were held at 12 noon and 3.30 pm. What most isitors paid their 1/- to see was the Prentice Pillar. The story is that the pillar was carved by an apprentice during the absence of his naster in Rome. On the return of the senior man, he was so jealous of the junior's work, that he killed him on the spot. Here Wilson ommandeers two local stonemasons to stage a tableau of the story. Quite which is playing the master and which the apprentice is ifficult to say as both look similar in age and experience!

AUL C2810x

DALKEITH

The Old Parish Church and Dalkeith drew visitors from Edinburgh. Things appear fairly quiet on this summer day c1880 with quite a crowd of men happily passing time by watching the photographer at work. The dog is the least interested participant. He would not last long nowadays if he were to lie in the same place despite the relative absence of traffic. The granite setts have gone as have the awnings on the shops and the bay window on number 83 but otherwise the scenes are remarkably similar.

PORTOBELLO

Portobello became a very popular destination for day-trippers from the city. Nicknamed 'Edinburgh Super Mare', its attractions included the fine sands, pier, boating and swimming. Here the beach is in full use. Bathing machines, all of which advertise Beecham's Pills, could be hired for 3d a day and a horse is at work to tow some to the water's edge to let the occupants enter the water discreetly. Children are digging or paddling under the watchful eye of their well dressed parents, and despite the stiff wind that has kept Henry's boats on the beach, the ice-cream and lemonade sellers are doing a good trade. Other trippers are in the promenade cafes, the Parisian and Continental.

A hundred years later, the beach is deserted and the facilities reduced to a funfair and a restaurant. The Tower which was built in 1785 for the lawyer John Cunninghame, still has the same spectacular views across the Forth, but otherwise Portobello has little left in common with its Victorian heyday. The excursionists go elsewhere these days, but if the Scottish summers heat up, who can tell what may happen?

Portobello and Newhaven both had piers to add to their attractions. Portobello's was demolished in 1917.

LEITH

Ten minutes away by tram from Princes Street, Leith in the nineteenth century was a separate burgh — the sixth largest in Scotland — and very proud of its identity. At the heart of Leith was the Old Harbour which holds an interesting mixture of shipping; a steamer called the Berlin, various lighters, a small puffer and beyond the swingbridge a paddle steamer bound up the Forth to Stirling. The customs house and old port which housed the headquarters of the Submarine Mariners (Forth Division) are replaced by attractive new housing, part of the regeneration of the whole waterside area which has taken place over the last decade. Familiar landmarks remain such as the Signal tower and Sailors' Home which was used by 2,500 men each year in the 1890's. The Water of Leith much less black and foul than it used to be.

LEITH PIER . 4574. G.W.W.

LEITH PIER

A tug tows out a large paddle steamer, perhaps one of the ferries to Fife while a Peterhead coaster manoeuvres in mid-channel. A favourite Victorian walk was to follow out one pier, catch the boat that plied between the pierheads and come back the other, a good two mile excursion. McGonogall visited Leith with predictable poetic results.

"And for the Docks, they are magnificent to see,
They compromise five docks, two piers, 1,141 yards long respectively,
And there's steamboat communication with London and the North of Scotland,
And the fares are really cheap and the accommodation most grand".

AUL C3315

LEITH DOCKS

Leith was a very busy port in Victorian times, handling large quantities of grain, timber and wine and some of that trade remain though the Victoria and the other docks are less busy. In 1898 there were nearly 200 steamers operating out of Leith. The bigges firm was James Currie and Company., and one of their sailing ships — the Svelvig — which was used in the Scandinavian trade ha its sails partially unfurled to allow the crew to do some patching. Wilson himself was a painter by early training and would certainl have stopped to look over the shoulder of this artist at work.

NEWHAVEN

...ate nineteenth century Newhaven was a thriving fishing village and home to a very distinct community which kept itself to itself, ...arely marrying outside. The men were mostly fishers though some worked as coopers or sailmakers and the women went out to ...Edinburgh and surrounding localities to sell the catch. Theirs was a picturesque dress to compensate in part for the harshness of ...heir lives, required as they were to carry their laden creels for miles with their cries of "caller haddies" or "caller herrings" ringing ...out, 'caller' being an old Scots word for 'fresh'. Purchasers were advised to haggle hard; "never give a fishwife the half of what she ...asks" was one saying. Notice how neatly the wifie is dressed in her blue jerkin, petticoat of red and yellow stripes, cap edged with ...lace and carefully polished boots. To judge from the footprints in the sand, George Washington Wilson has taken some time to ...move her into position.

Fish curers in Newhaven today have a different style of dress — wellyboots and overalls — which is no longer peculiar to their ...occupation or locality. Behind them the harbour holds more pleasure craft than fishing boats.

TRINITY PIER, NEWHAVEN

ike many other seaside resorts in Britain, Newhaven had a pier. It was built in 1821 by Captain Brown of the Royal Navy, the itention being to attract coastal steamers and so boost the trade of Newhaven. For a while the pier was quite successful but the ompletion of nearby Granton drew off virtually all the traffic. The Fife ferry, for instance transferred in September 1844 and few ruises thereafter bothered to call at Newhaven. Swimmers and walkers used the pier but it had become very rickety by 1914. At ιe landward end however its existence is not forgotten.

NEWHAVEN MAIN STREET

Sensibly and sympathetically restored in the 1960's the Main Street retains much of the atmosphere caught in Wilson'
photograph. There are still outside stairs and cobbles, and the hardware store and the pub across the road remain. What is gone '
the pervasive smell of fish and mussels which Victorian visitors found so pronounced.

CRAMOND BRIDGE

BELOW CRAMOND BRIDGE

The new (1823) bridge across the Almond had long since taken away most of the traffic which had once used the old bridge. It still needs repair as it had done before in 1617, 1687, 1761, 1776 and 1854. The setting is as attractive as before and the walk down to Cramond village as popular as ever but there are no working mills to be seen. Traces of lades and ponds which cost millers so much effort to maintain can be located without too much difficulty as at Downie's Mills.

WARSHIPS IN THE FORTH

In June 1860 the Channel Fleet anchored off Queensferry for a two week visit and undeterred by a rumour that some of the sailo had smallpox thousands of spectators came out from Edinburgh. Some embarked at Leith or Granton on paddle steamers an enterprising fishermen chartered out their boats for a day. A medley of craft can be seen round the flagship **Royal Albert** whi had been designed as a sailing ship but modified during construction to have auxiliary steam power. Over a thousand men live on her which explains why the fear of infectious disease was very real indeed. Made obsolete by the arrival of ironclads after th American Civil War, she was sold off in 1883.

A cruiser and three sloops lie in the Forth off South Queensferry. A pinnace is making for Port Edgar harbour but the railwa company's timber jetty stands deserted, it being no longer required for the shipment of materials to the Bridge which it had serve To the west is the very elderly Caledonia, a veteran of the Napoleonic War which was being used as a training ship: she was hom to 700 boys. Behind her there is no sign of work having begun on the naval base at Rosyth, plans for which wer announced in 1903.

H.M.S. Edinburgh, here seen on the Fife side was a turret warship built in 1882. A make and mend day appears to be in progre and the washing is draped over the quarter deck rails. She was not the first Royal Navy ship to carry the name, nor the last. The was the small ship belonging to the Scottish navy which was transferred to the Royal Navy in 1707 and sunk two years later to act a a breakwater at Harwich. The cruiser H.M.S. Edinburgh which was launched in 1938 was torpedoed four years later in the Baren Sea; her cargo of gold was recently salvaged.

WARSHIPS ABOVE THE FORTH BRIDGE, OFF QUEENSFERRY.   II.243.   G.W.W.

FORTH BRIDGE

Work on the Railway Bridge across the Forth started in 1883. It immediately became a major attraction and tens of thousands visitors came to South Queensferry to watch the progress of construction during the next seven years. Some came by speci charabanc from Princes Street, others by rail to Dalmeny Station and yet others by steamer from Leith which allowed an inspectic of the works at Inchgarvie destroyed by fire in February 1889. The Fife ferries left from the slipway below the Bridge but they wer out of business when the Road Bridge was opened in 1964, to the great relief of many who had to queue in the summer months or t go round by Kincardine.